HRJC

D1289333

DIEGO FORLÁN

TO THE TOP!

2011 Announces that he will be playing for Inter PF starting on August 29th.

2010 During May and June, plays in the South Africa World Cup. Wins the Balon d'Or on June 11th

2009 Wins the Golden Shoe for a second time

2007 Joins Atlético FC of Madrid, starting on June 30th.

2005 Nominated Special Amassidor of UNICEF on May 22. Wins the Golden Shoe.

2004 Starts for Villareal on October 30th.

2002 In June he plays for his national team in the Korea-Japan World Cup. Plays his first game for Manchester United on October 29th.

1998 Debuts in Independientes on October 25th

1993 Joins the junior squad for Peñarol Club in September.

1979 Diego Martín Forlán Corazo born on may 19th.

ISBN-13: 978-1-4222-2665-0 (hc) — 978-1-4222-9206-8 (ebook)

Printing (last digit) 9 8 7 6 5 4 3 2 1
Printed and bound in the United States of America.
CPSIA Compliance Information: Batch #S2013. For further information, contact Mason Crest at 1-866-MCP-Book.

About the Author: Daniel John Grady is a Chilean author. He is from Chiloé, an island in the Chilean Patagonia. As an economist, he has published several articles in national newspapers. As part of his commitment to helping his community, he is a volunteer fire-fighter and arson investigator.

Photo credits: EFE/Paolo Aguilar: 4; EFE/David Ebener: 25; EFE/Iván Franco: 7; EFE / Lavandeira jr / pdm: 13; Shutterstock.com: 1, 2, 10, 11, 14, 16, 17, 20, 23, 26, 28; UNICEF: 29; Wikimedia: 8.

TABLE OF CONTENTS

Uruguay's Diego Forlan holds the trophy with teammates after winning the Copa America final soccer match against Paraguay in Buenos Aires, July 24, 2011.

 **CHAPTER 1**

Uruguay's Top Scorer

ON JULY 10TH, 2010 THE PEOPLE OF URUGUAY watched the World Cup semifinal in South Africa wth growing anticipation. The score was even at one against Germany, and two Uruguayan players were rapidly approaching the opposite goal. The entire country held its breath, and then Diego Folán scored what would later be called the best goal of the World Cup.

While Uruguay took the lead at that point, in the end it would be Germany who took home the victory. However, Diego Forlán's exceptional performance, both in that game and in the previous matches, won him enough admiration to be awarded the Balon d'Or. This is the highest distinction that that a player can achieve during the World Cup.

The prize was one more in a series of Diego's exceptional achievements: he is the player with the most games under his belt of this national team. He has the record of highest scores and he'd already achieved two Golden Boot trophies during his time playing in European Football

Known throughout the continent

As the other Latin American teams were eliminated from the World Cup, Latin football fans began to support what would ultimately be the only country from the continent to dispute a spot

Diego Forlán is currently an honorary member of Peñarol Club, a distinction that is given to world-class sports players who started their career there.

on the podium. The Uruguayan success was so unexpected because it's such a small country, surrounded by football giants such as Argentina and Brazil.

The triumph of the "carruas" fostered goodwill and support from many of the people in South America, making Diego Forlán a common and well-known name on the continent. This acknowledgement was repeated the next year when Diego led his team to victory in the Argentina 2011 America's Cup. In fact, he scored two of the three winning goals in the final game, and brought home the trophy. Afterwards he commented, "It means a lot. My grandfather won it, my father won it, and now I have won it. Three generations that have won it. It's a proud moment for the family." He was referring to Juan Carlos Corazo and his father.

Not only did he win accolades on the field, but when he was still only 25 years old he was nominated as special embassi-dor by UNICEF to help the impoverished children of his country and the continent. It's representative of his personality, being committed to helping others.

The hero's origins

Diego Martín Forlán Corazo—also known as "Cachabacha"—was born on May 19, 1979, in Montevideo, the capital of Uruguay. His father was Pablo Forlán who had already played for the Uruguayan national football team. His maternal grandfather Juan Carlos Corazo was a famous team manager for the national team who was in charge of the team for their push for the Chile '62 World Cup. Diego surprised a lot of people, then, when as a child he decided to play tennis. He was very enthusiastic with the sport, and still plays today. But when he turned 14 he finally decided to follow his father's footsteps and commit himself to football.

Some time before that, his family went through a tragedy: his sister, Alejandra,

The Charrúas are the native people of what is now Uruguay. The name is used often to refer to people of Uruguayan origin, irrespective of their heritage.

(Opposite page) Diego with his sister, Alejandra (seated in a wheelchair) and their father, Pablo. The Alejandra Forlan Foundation in Montevideo is a charity which works to prevent traffic accidents and contributes to the rehabilitation of victims of vehicle accidents.

Diego's grandfather, Juan Carlos Corazo, was a professional football player in Argentina during the 1930s. He was also the manager of the Uruguayan national team in their bid for the 1962 World Cup.

who was only 10 years old at the time, was in a serious car accident which caused her to lose the use of her legs. Considering the high costs of rehabilitation, the English press speculated that Diego decided to play football to help his sister.

What is true is that when he turned 14, his football career blossomed. He started playing in the youth squad of the Danubio Football Club of Montevideo. Soon after he joined the Peñarol Athletic Club, which

is by itself is a significant achievemen, even considering he was the son of a famous football player. The Peñarol club—also known as the Aurinegros in Spanish, because of the gold and black colors of their uniforms—is a world-class team, and consequently selects its rookies with lots of care. In 1999, their team was named the best in Latin America during the 20th century. This legacy was the starting point of Diego's football career.

The first steps

His stay in the first teams was short. Having finished playing in the junior league, he crossed the River Plate to Argentina to join Independientes de Avellaneda, a strong professional Argentine team. That's where he debuted in the first division on October 25, 1998, while he was still only 17 years old. He was praised for his distinguished participation in the Copa del Ray (King's Cup), and from there his football skill only grew.

What he didn't know during the championship was that an important person in world football was watching intently. Quite soon after Diego got a telephone call from Sir Alex Ferguson, the manager of Manchester United, a very powerful English football club. His world would be turned on its head.

Aside from soccer, Diego plays golf and tennis.

CHAPTER 2

The Great Leap

DIEGO FORLÁN WAS BARELY 22 YEARS OLD when he stepped on the pitch for the first time in the England's Premier League, next to football stars like David Beckham. In fact, the first goal he scored in England was a penalty after a foul against Beckham. However, his time in Manchester was both sweet and sour.

Diego signed for the Red Devils—as the team from Old Trafford is known to its fans—after the manager's brother, Martin Ferguson, saw his skill level in Argentina. The field change did not worry Diego, as he commented later: "Even before I landed in Manchester I spoke with Alex Ferguson and we understood each other completely. And when I landed for the first time, the press was waiting for me. There was a surprise press conference where I answered all their questions in English, even though I was a bit nervous."

He had good reason to be nervous. Even though his first game was on January 29th, it wasn't until eight months later that he would claim his first score.

He explained himself in this way: "Obviously I arrived at a big team, with big players, so getting into the team as a starter wasn't easy. There was Van Nistelrooy, York, Cole, Giggs, Soljskaer . . . Not having so many chances to start and coming into the game from the bench, my game time was little." The trouble was, he didn't play for a whole game. He would join the field in the last minutes of the game when the team was pulling back on the throttle and there was little chance to score. "I could only learn and keep growing whenever I could," he said.

Sir Alex Furguson has been manger of Manchester United for over 25 years, making him the longest serving manager in the history of the club.

Getting noticed

His first opportunity to score came on October 22, 2002, when Manchester United was playing against Aston Villa. Until then, Diego had acquired the nickname "Diego Forlorn" on account of his goals being "as rare as diamonds."

The English team was running out of time and the fans were watching with growing dread as the scoreboard stayed decisively against them. Suddenly Diego appeared with a swift hard kick and scored the equalizing goal, bringing cheer and finally celebration for the team and its followers.

Diego's relationship with the fans had more to do with his charisma than his work on the field. His teammates remember him as a simple man with a generous heart. He was not interested in fame or superfluous things. He was committed to the game and had zero attraction to luxury. But he was also fast approaching a decisive moment for his team, where he would save the day.

Fan favorite

Diego finally managed to conquer the hearts of the Red Devils on December 1, 2002, against their archrival Liverpool. And to make the situation more significant, Manchester was playing as the visiting team. They really needed to win that game, and it was Diego who scored both goals to win the match. He recalled later, "It wasn't an easy game to start in, and in the first half it was very difficult. Part of me thought they were going to sub me out, but everything changed in the second half." The team's captain, Gary Neville, approached him after the game saying, "They'll never forget you after that." And so it was.

Even years later when Diego had already moved on from Manchester, he was still remembered by the fans. They had a chant: "He comes from Uruguay, and he makes the Scousers cry." The Scousers is the nickname for Liverpool, and Diego gets misty eyes when he hears it being sung by the fans while watching a game on television. His time with the Red Devils had more downs than ups, but in the end, is greatest conquest were the hearts of the fans. He still watches Manchester U's games.

But nothing lasts forever. Diego was spending most of his time on the sidelines instead of in the field. He said, "there came a time, when I was 24 years old, when I only wanted to play, prove what I was worth, so I wanted to get off the sidelines and had to leave the club." Things like that are never simple, of course, and his record was starting to worry the manager.

A falling out

During the four years he played for Manchester, he scored 17 times. He was with the team when it won the Premiere League in the 2002-03 season, and the FA Cup in 2003-04. But Fate had decided to send him in another direction, and it was time to put an end to his time in England.

When the 2004-05 season started, Forlan played in nine games without managing to score. On August 15, 2004, Manchester United was playing the first game of the season against Chelsea, one of the favorites to win the Cup. The manager, Sir Alex, it seemed was losing his patience

Manchester United is a cultural icon in the United Kingdom, and its rivalry with Liverpool is legendary.

While Diego Forlán played for them, Manchester United was one of the most popular soccer clubs in the world. It was also one of the most valuable, with an estimated net worth of $1.6 billion.

player nodded, but when he was at his locker he instead decided to wear his favorite medium-studded shoes. Shortly after, he was staring down the goalie with an easy shot which would have saved the Red Devils from defeat. But Diego slipped on the ground. The manager realized what had happened, and was so angry with Diego that he picked up the shoes and threw them at him. Sir Alex is not the sort of man who forgives quickly, and that was the end of Diego Forlán in Manchester United.

and the Uruguayan had to do everything to save his career.

Then it started raining. The manager instructed Diego to wear shoes with long studs to deal with the slippery ground. The

Generally, the football teams of each country are grouped in leagues to play in domestic tournaments. A league is a grouping of clubs that choose a regulating body and define certain rules. Normally, the leagues are further divided into divisions, one of higher category (major) and one of lower standing (minor). Many divisions have their own names which are fairly well-known. The teams of each division play against each other, scoring points and the team with the most points is crowned the winner. The teams with the most points go on to play in international tournaments, and those with too few points drop to the lower division. Meanwhile the clubs will often play a knock-off tournament which disputes a cup. Some leagues are very popular and have a world-wide following, which allows them to draft the best players. Among them are the Premier League (England), La Liga (Spain), Serie A (Italy) and Bundesliga (Germany). Diego Forlán played in three of these.

Manuel Pablo of Deportivo cannot stop the incursion of Manchester United's Diego Forlan during their Champions League match in 2003.

Villareal FC's greatest triumph was during the first year that Diego Forlán played for them. They reached the semifinals of the UEFA Champions League, which brings together the best teams of Europe.

CHAPTER 3

Villareal vs. Atlético

AFTER HIS TIME IN THE ENGLISH FOOTBALL LEAGUES, 2004 was a year of change for Diego Forlan. First was a field change: he was called to play for Villareal, a Spanish team managed by another South American. Manuel Pellegrini was a new manager for the team, and was much more in tune with the Uruguayan player.

"The Villareal of the time wasn't like it is now, respected in Spain and known in Europe," Diego commented later about the change. "At that time I was taking a step down, but I knew I was going to a team that was doing things the right way and wanted to grow . . . Going to play for Villareal was like taking a step back to later take two forward."

And what steps he made! In his first year playing for Villareal, he achieved his first major award. The very prestigious sports Spanish sports magazine *Marca* nominated him the season's "Pichichi." It's a special acknowledgement that is given to the highest scorer of the Spanish League. He achieved it with 25 goals scored. Those same goals gave him the Golden Shoe, which he shared with Thierry Henry. The Golden Shoe is given to the highest scoring player in Europe.

Top Scorer

Of the 25 goals scored by Diego Forlán en in the 2004-05 season in the Spanish League, 23 were with kicks and only one with the head. "I came to Spain to go back to playing football and have fun. It's incredible all I've accomplished," he announced. The numbers are also impressive for the team,

standards. The club is known as the "Yellow Submarine"—Submarino Amarillo in Spanish—because of the color of its jerseys and because it's a low-profile club compared to it's rivals.

After all, it is surrounded by famous teams which call Valencia home as well, Real Madrid and Barcelona PC, which at that time had the best soccer player in the world: Ronaldinho. Villareal's adversaries regularly sported the best players in Europe and the World, and it was against them that Diego would have to play.

However, the change of teams was part of Chachabacha's strategy. While playing for Manchester United, he had few opportunities to actually play, because he was only called on the field as a substitute. This meant he had few chances to score. In an emerging club like Villareal, Diego would play as a starter. That way he would play for the whole game and show his real qualities as a player.

The effort to remain

Diego's debut in the Primera Liga (Premier League) was pretty impressive. His most memorable match was against Barcelona, the team that had suffered the fewest losses during the season. Reaching the goalie to have a chance to score was the biggest challenge for any forward in the League for that season, because Barcelona had such a strong defense. In game number 37 of the season, Villareal was up against this formidable adversary. The match ended with the scoreboard tied at 3; with Diego Forlán

Manuel Pellegrini was a Chilean manager of Villareal PF between 2004 and 2009 when Diego played with the team.

because before he arrived, the highest season scorer was Victor Fernandez with just 24 goals.

Villareal is a football club from the Spanish city with the same name. It's located in the Valencia Community. The city itself has only 40,000 inhabitants, and it's team is considered a small one by La Liga

As a starting striker for Villareal, Diego had many chances to score.

scoring a stunning hat trick. Scoring three consecutive goals against Barcelona was unheard of in the League. This achievement wouldn't be repeated for years.

By 2006 things became more difficult for Diego. He suffered a series of injuries and sprains which left him unable to play at his top level. And after a year with so many impressive achievements it was hard for him to beat his own record. He no longer was measured against other players; his objective now was to beat the records he himself had established. It would take some time.

Paying back

Not everything was soccer. Diego is also a human being, and makes mistakes in the same way he achieves. He knows how to rise to a challenge, but also knows how to give a hand to help out. On May 22, 2005, he was nominated as UNICEF's special Ambassador to Uruguay. UNICEF is a United Nations fund for helping impoverished children. It brings together famous people from around the world to raise awareness to the difficulties underprivileged children face. It is one of the many forms that Diego has to help his country.

"He's a role model for children and teenagers, the ideal person to promote the organization's message in the country and around the world," is what the head of the UNICEF office in Uruguay, Anne Beathe Jensen, had to say about Diego.

During the nomination ceremony that was held in Montevideo, Diego spoke to the gathered children, many of whom wanted to be just like him. "I will try to do everything I can to keep supporting your rights, so you are cared for more and have a happy childhood," he said.

Even though he's very passionate about this activity, it's not the only charity organization he spends his time with. Forlan uses the fame his sports achievements has created to help other people. He works with and spends an enormous amount of time working with his sister's foundation. Alejandra Forlán, his sister who suffered a crippling accident, runs the foundation to help prevent traffic accidents and rehabilitate their victims.

The Pichichi Trophy is awarded annually. It is administered by a Spanish sports magazine called *Marca* (Score). Journalists from the periodical count and compare the number of goals each player makes, and from that come up with a winner. The statistics are from the journalists' own observations, and not from the official record. Because of this, sometimes there are discrepancies with the number of goals. The prize is for the player of the First Division of the Spanish Soccer League (La Liga) who scores the most goals during a season.

The name is a tribute to Rafael Moreno Aranzadi, whose nickname was Pichichi. He played for Athletic and became famous between 1910 and 1920 because of his goal-scoring record. This was before the league was created.

> **The Athletic Club of Madrid (Club Atlético de Madrid), where Diego started playing in 2006, is one of the founders of the Spanish League, where it started in the first division.**

In that vein, Alejandra commented, "I always say that seeing someone from afar and admiring them is easy. But knowing him close, like I know him, with his virtues and his flaws, and to keep admiring him has a very special meaning."

Back in soccer

In 2006 Diego achieved another record by scoring 40 goals in the yellow jersey, becoming the most successful striker in Villareal's history.

After three years with the Yellow Submarine, 2007 brought a new change. The Atlético Madrid club bought him from Villareal for 9 million Euros plus Luis Perea, one of the most expensive transfers in Spanish football to date.

Atlético is, as its name says, a team from Madrid, Spain. It's a rival to Real Madrid. The team and its fans are known as "los colchoneros," or the mattress makers, and they have a very long track record of accomplishments, even before Diego arrived. Their colors are horizontal white and red stripes which gives them the more known nickname of "rojiblacos."

"It was a dream debut," was how Diego described his first game with the Madrid team. It was a match against Gloria Bistra, a Romanian team of their Division A, and they were both trying to qualify for the UEFA Cup. Diego scored the first and only goal of the game, bringing home the victory for his team.

Return to England

Atlético gave Diego a second chance to return to England and measure himself against his old rivals in the Premier League. In February 2008, Atlético was up against Bolton Wanderers still vying for the UEFA Cup. However, English soil once again slipped under Diego's feet, and his team had to go home without scoring.

A few months later, however, Diego achieved another title. On April 6th 2008, his team was up against Almería and he scored his 68th goal, becoming the highest scoring Uruguayan in the Spanish League.

The 2007-08 season was very fruitful for Diego, even though he didn't achieve any prizes. He scored 23 times, creating a formidable team alongside Argentine striker Sergio Agüero.

The next year he managed to repeat his score from his first year at Villareal, but this time in red and white: First, he was nominated for the Pichichi award of the year as the highest scoring player of the League. Later, he was awarded the Golden Boot as the highest scoring player in Europe.

It was time to hang up his club jersey and put on his country's colors. The biggest challenge for any soccer player was just around the corner.

Uruguayan football fans watch the game between Uruguay and Holland during the 2010 South Africa World Cup on a huge television screen erected in the center of Montevideo. Behind the screen you can see a statue of José Gervasio Artigas (1764-1850), founder of Uruguay.

CHAPTER 4

The World Cup

THE WORLD CUP DRAWS THE BEST SOCCER PLAYERS on the planet, representing their respective countries. Their country's glory and honor is in play, under the watchful eyes of the world. And for the players there is a special prize: the Balón d'Or which is given to the best player of the tournament. During the South Africa 2010 Cup, that player was Diego Forlán.

Diego's first international match was back in 2002. He still hadn't received the fateful call to join the English soccer league, but his talent playing for Independientes already won him a spot on the Uruguayan national team which would play in the Korea-Japan World Cup.

As in any country which manages to be selected to dispute the World Cup, there was a lot of hope both in the people of Uruguay and in the players. But this wasn't the time of the Charrúas.

The first game was lost to Denmark, and the young Forlán didn't even play. After that, the team was able to hold its own against what was at the time the world champion, France. They managed a hard-fought draw. In the next match, everything seemed lost when Diego Forlán stepped on the pitch for the first time. Uruguay was down by three goals against Senegal. Before the stunned eyes of the crowd, Diego managed to score a goal, then another! There was hope in the team still. But even though they managed to score three goals, it wasn't enough to go on to the second round.

However, this gave Diego experience on the world pitch. After that, he'd always be a starter for the Uruguayan national team.

Intermission

While Cachabacha managed a string of successes in Europe, his national team wasn't doing so well. The scene was fairly discouraging during the play-offs for the Germany 2006 Wold Cup. Diego only played in the last few games, and Uruguay did not manage to be selected. The loss hit Diego particularly hard, especially since he'd already played in a World Cup. However, he had no other option but to support his neighbors, saying, "I have a lot of affection for Argentina. Since we can't be there, I will be putting all my heart in them."

During the Americas Cup of 2007, Uruguay fell in the first round against the team that would eventually win: Brazil. Even though during the game Diego managed to score a goal, during the penalty round he lost his shot, and Uruguay's hope vanished with the scoreboard showing a 5-4 score against them.

The preparation

As soon as the Americas Cup was finished, the first round of playoffs for the South Africa 2010 World Cup started. On October 13, 2007, Uruguay beat Bolivia by a broad margin, making many of the fans wonder where that energy was while the team was trying to achieve the cup. However, after that, things were hardly any different than the run-up to the 2002 World Cup.

Uruguay again managed to be selected, just barely as the last team on the list, and only after narrowly winning the rebound match against Costa Rica. There was more wishing than hope when it came to predicting the results of the World Cup.

Uruguay's official name is "República Oriental del Uruguay," or Eastern Republic of Uruguay. There are just over three million people living there. Its national team has the most official prizes and trophies of any national team in the world. They have won 15 Americas Cups, 2 World Cups, 2 Olympic games, and one Golden Cup. Diego was of course correct when he said that soccer is very important in Uruguay, and that fact is reflected in the national squad's trophy collection. The squad was the first to play an international tournament outside of the British Isles, losing 3-2 to Argentina. They were also the first continental champions of the first Americas Cup in 1916.

Their most notable achievements were in 1924 and 1928 when Uruguay won the Gold Medal during the Olympic Games. These were the only Olympic tournaments which were organized by FIFA, and recognized as World Championships. When the first World Cup was disputed in 1930, Uruguay became the first World Champion. In 1950 the squad managed to win again, becoming four-times world champions. They are only surpassed by Brazil.

Currently, FIFA ranks Uruguay's national team fourth in the world.

In 2010, however, something happened. Uruguay played two friendly matches before the World Cup, winning on both occasions. Neither Switzerland nor Israel were able to beat the Charruas, and some analysts started to look at the Uruguayan team with new eyes. Hope was reborn, but cautious hope it still was. However, it was 2010 and by then the team had a player who had won two Golden Boots.

Uruguay's national squad traditionally plays with light blue jerseys since 1910, when they won their first international tournament in Montevideo.

Hope is reborn

During the sorting, Uruguay was put into Group A along with the host country, South Africa. The other teams were Mexico and France. Against the latter Uruguay would play first, with Diego Forlán starting as striker.

The World Cup championship is divided into two phases. The 32 participating countries are sorted into 8 groups of four. The

Diego celebrates a goal for Uruguay's national team.

The Fédération Internationale de Football Association (FIFA) has 208 member countries which participate in their tournaments. That is 16 more countries than the United Nations.

teams of in each group play against each other in turn, adding points. For each game they win, they get three points; for each drawn match, they get one point; and each loss counts for zero points.

In the first game where Diego would play, the results didn't do anything but confirm the expectations of those who thought this would be a repeat of 2002. France and Uruguay once again ended in a draw with zero scores. The players left the field downcast.

Things couldn't stay like that, however. Three days later, Uruguay was to play South Africa, and at the 24 minute marker Diego scored the first goal. He wasn't happy with just that, and at minute 80 he managed the decisive goal that would mean the first international win for Uruguay in the World Cup tournament. The scoreboard would finish at 3-0 with another goal by Alvaro Pereira in overtime.

It was six days later when the rest of Latin America woke up and took none of the small team wearing light blue jerseys: They beat Mexico by one goal, taking the top of the group's ranking and knocking the host country out of the competition. Uruguay was in the finals.

Fighting for the top

Not everything is on the scoreboard, of course. Teamwork is fundamental, and so is sportsmanship. With this in mind Diego and his striker teammate Luis Suarez coordinated their plays in such a way that they would be recognized as the most formidable duo of the encounter. In the first game of the finals, it was Suarez who scored. In the next game it was Forlán's turn.

The fateful moment came on June 6, 2010, when Uruguay was playing the semifinals against Holland, and Diego was playing without his wingman. He tried to work with Maximiliano Pereira, but the Dutch team kept the ball for much of the time. Thus, they managed to score one more goal than the light blue team. When the clock was at 73 minutes, Arjen Robben finished off the dreams of the small country from the borders of the River Plate.

There was a final ray of hope: the match for third place against Germany.

A successful failure

There were two major events during the game against Germany. First, the Germans managed to score three times against the Charruas. But Uruguay had more than

Diego Forlán is currently the Uruguayan national team's top scoring striker with 32 goals, and with the most games played (84).

Diego was selected as the best player of the 2010 World Cup tournament.

enough reason to celebrate. The second event was that the best goal belonged to their team. The Forlán-Suarez duo scored what was broadly recognized as the best goal of the World Cup tournament. Not only that, during the winning ceremony, Diego Forlán was given the extremely prestigious Balón d'Or as the best player of the World Cup.

Of course it wasn't the same as bringing home the World Cup, but the recognition and the team's achievement was enough to inspire the Uruguayan people to give the warmest of welcomes when their team came home. "In Uruguay, I remember as a little boy, there is no other game except soccer," said Diego. And the recognition his country bestowed upon him shows that.

The 2010 World Cup was an important moment in Diego's life, but naturally not the only one. When the national teams went home, Diego went back to play for his Club. His private life suffered changes as well. The national team will always be there to call him when needed. But his passion is playing soccer, and until the next World Cup, he will do what he does best: play football.

Diego Forlán is currently one of the best strikers in the world. Here he is in the red and white jersey of Villareal.

CHAPTER 5

New Challenges

THERE WERE MANY CHANGES in Diego's life during 2011. In the soccer world, Diego began playing for Inter Milan, one of the best-known teams on the planet. In his personal life, however, the three-year relationship with his fiancée came to an end. Her name is Zaira Nara, and she is a model from Argentina. Certainly it's not easy to be a superstar.

Diego Forlán recognizes that he is a Twitter fan. He has over 1.2 million followers. "It gives you the chance to tell people things that intrigue us all," he explains. Of course, on the other hand, "often there is a lot of information that's not true." But he sincerely cares about having contact with his football fans, and social networks offer a unique opportunity to do so.

However, there is one thing where social networks haven't helped him out much. At first, it was good news: in march 2011, Diego announced through Twitter that he was going to marry Zaira Nara, an Argentine fashion model. They had been dating for over three years, and it only confirmed what the foot-

baller and model's followers had been anticipating for some time.

It was quite a surprise later in June, however, when both announced that they were putting an end to their relationship. And that was it. The cause for their breakup is mostly speculation; neither have given any reason why they wouldn't continue together. Nothing more than say they are happy and wish each other the best

It's true that there are rumors of other possible romantic interests, but only time will tell how true they are. We can only wait for confirmation from

Diego's official Twitter feed.

Professionally

His personal problems don't seem to be affecting Diego's football playing. Barely a month after the breakup, he was playing in the 2010 Americas Cup in Argentina. This time the Uruguayan national team had the honor of taking home the trophy. During the championship, Diego became the highest scorer in his country's history. And considering he still plays on the national team, we can expect him to keep breaking his own record in the upcoming championships.

> **Diego Forlán is Catholic, though "not one to go to church often." He believes in "thanking instead of asking" when he prays.**

Also, he was inducted as an honorary member of Peñarol Sporting Club, the team where he started his career.

However, the biggest news in his career is that in August 2011 he was transferred to Inter Milan, one of the most powerful teams on the planet. There was some serious negotiations before the transfer, with a great many teams showing interest in hav-

In August 2011, Diego left Madrid's Athletic FC and joined Inter Milan, a famous Italian football club.

UNICEF stands for United Nations International Children's Emergency Fund. It was created in 1946 to deliver food and humanitarian assistance to children in countries devastated by World War II. In 1953 it became a permanent part of the United Nations with a new name, United Nations Children's Fund, but its original initials persist to this day. It is financed by donations from individuals and governments. Its programs focus on developing community-level services to give support to children in need. In 1965 UNICEF won the Nobel Peace Prize for its work. Diego Forlán has been the fund's spokesperson in Uruguay since 2005, and considers it an important part of his life.

ing him on their side. "This is a superlative player. It's hard to find a player with so much success," was how the president of Atlético described the situation. It was part of his farewell speech before Diego left his team.

And what does Diego think of his time in the "rojiblanco"? "They were four years of victories and losses, but what lasts is the human touch, what remains when it's over."

Diego feels like he's in a privileged position in his news club and new city. "I'm in the center of Europe. It's possible to go lots of places. It's easier than it was in Madrid," he said, speaking of the change. A new soccer season in Europe is starting, and Diego is returning from two years of success. Sometimes staying on the top is harder than getting there.

Projects

Not everything can be soccer. Diego is still very enthusiastic about his work as Ambassador for UNICEF in Uruguay. "He likes to be with the kids. Any time he can he goes to their school and we bring along other football players to meet them. It's a special treat for the kids," his father, Pablo, explains, while helping him with his social work.

Diego is also inaugurating a line of infant products, and a percentage of the profit from them will be given to underprivileged children in the country.

During the negotiations which eventually ended with his transfer to Inter Milan, Diego's father said that Málaga's manager was very interested in his son

Also he keeps active in his sister's foundation trying to prevent traffic accidents. Not only does he use the fame he's acquired as a football player to raise awareness and help people: it's also a good opportunity to try out his other sporting skills.

He says he's an avid reader when time allows. He particularly likes historical novels and biographies. He never stopped playing tennis, and he has several friends who are professional tennis players. Frequently he plays with them for fun.

His biggest source of pride, however, is combining all the above to help other people in need. For example, he organizes a charity golf tournament where he will play along with other sporting legends such as Argentine golfer Andrés Romero and the Chilean footballer Iván Zamorano.

What's coming

In the football world, for now Diego is concerned with training with his new team. He already has signed on with the Uruguayan national squad to participate in the playoffs for the Brazil 2014 World Cup. After that, he has another shot at the Americas Cup. He has a lot of football ahead, and we also hope a lot of success as well.

Zaira Tatiana Nara, now Diego's ex-fiancée, was born in Bolougne, Argentina on August 15, 1988. She began her modeling career when she was very young as a child model with her sister, Wanda. She currently works as an anchorwoman in Argentina, as well as being one of the most sought-after models for advertising in her country. She has worked for two Argentine television channels: El Trece and Telefe. A major accomplishment in her career is to have been the face of a world-wide Pantene commercial. She met Diego at a celebrity party in Punta del Este, and they texted for several months before starting a relationship. She hasn't given a reason for the break-up either.

FURTHER READING

Alvarez, Luciano. "History of Peñarol" Montevideo: Alvarez, 2005.

Brotons, Pablo. "The Story of Atlético de Madrid" Madrid: Prime Books, 2010.

Forlán, Diego. "Uruguayo" Montevideo: Editorial El Tercer Nombre, 2010.

Prats, Luis. "The Celeste Chronicle" Montevideo: Fin de Siglo, 2011.

Singer, Marcelo. "Closer to Heaven" Montevideo: Zona Editorial, 2010.

Villarejo, Luis. "Captains" Madrid: LID, 2010.

INTERNET RESOURCES

www.diegoforlan.com

Official website of Diego Forlan, with news about his latest activities, pictures, and more information about his life and interests.

twitter.com/diegoforlan7

Twitter account of Diego Forlán, where he posts his latest news and his views on various topics.

www.fundacionalejandraforlan.org

Official site of the Alejandra Forlan Foundation, which is dedicated to helping victims of traffic accidents.

www.fifa.com

Official site of the governing body of soccer activities worldwide. It has links to news, information on the World Cup, videos, and team rankings.

www.auf.org.uy

Official site of the Uruguayan Football Association, with information about the national team, internal tournaments, leagues, and other things.

INDEX